On the Front Lines

The U.S. Air Force at War

by Terri Sievert

Consultant:
Thomas J. Evelyn
Lieutenant Colonel, Aviation
U.S. Army

CAPSTONE
HIGH-INTEREST
BOOKS

an imprint of Capstone Press
Mankato, Minnesota

Capstone High-Interest Books are published by Capstone Press
151 Good Counsel Drive, P.O. Box 669, Mankato, Minnesota 56002
http://www.capstone-press.com

Library of Congress Cataloging-in-Publication Data
Sievert, Terri.
    U.S. Air Force at war/by Terri Sievert.
    p. cm.—(On the front lines)
    Includes bibliographical references and index.
    ISBN 0-7368-0921-X
    1. United States. Air Force—Juvenile literature. 2. United States.
Air Force—History—20th century—Juvenile literature. [1. United States.
Air Force.] I. Title. II. Series.
UG633 .S493 2002
358.4'00973—dc21   2001000445

Summary: Gives an overview of the U.S. Air Force, its mission, members,
history, recent conflicts, and modern equipment.

Editorial Credits

Blake Hoena, editor; Karen Risch, product planning editor; Steve Christensen,
    cover designer and illustrator; Katy Kudela, photo researcher

Photo Credits

AFFTC History Office, 27
Defense Visual Information Center, cover, 4, 7, 8, 10, 13, 14, 16, 19, 22–23,
    24, 29

1 2 3 4 5 6 07 06 05 04 03 02

Table of Contents

Chapter 1   The U.S. Air Force 5

Chapter 2   Air Force History 11

Chapter 3   Recent Conflicts 17

Chapter 4   Today's Air Force 25

Features

Important Dates. 21

B-2 Spirit 22

Women in the Air Force 27

Words to Know 30

To Learn More. 31

Useful Addresses. 31

Internet Sites 32

Index. 32

CHAPTER 1

Learn about:

- The Air Force mission

- Air Force members

- Air Force jobs

Some U.S. pilots flew F-117A Nighthawks during the Gulf War.

The U.S. Air Force

In 1990, the Middle East country of Iraq invaded Kuwait. The United States and other countries wanted to free Kuwait from Iraqi control. They sent troops to the area. These actions led to the Gulf War (1991).

On January 17, 1991, U.S. Air Force pilots flew F-117A Nighthawks into Iraq. Iraqi soldiers did not know these jet fighters were overhead. Nighthawks are specially designed to avoid being spotted by enemy forces.

Pilots dropped bombs on Baghdad. This city is the capital of Iraq. Pilots used smart bombs during their attacks. Crews aboard airplanes aim these bombs as they fall toward enemy targets. The pilots bombed factories, power plants, and military buildings.

Pilots also destroyed enemy communications equipment with bombs. This action made it difficult for Iraqi forces to talk with each other.

The Nighthawk pilots helped the United States and its allies defeat Iraq. Allies are countries that are friendly with one another.

U.S. Air Force

The Nighthawk pilots were members of the U.S. Air Force. The Air Force uses aircraft to protect the United States.

People volunteer to serve in the U.S. military. People who join the Air Force can be enlisted members or officers. Enlisted members are called airmen. Officers have more training than airmen. Officers also direct airmen in their duties.

Air Force Members

Air Force members can serve on active duty or in the reserves. Active duty members work full time for the Air Force. More than 350,000 people are active members of the Air Force. This number includes more than 280,000 enlisted members. Almost 70,000 active Air Force members are officers.

Members in the reserves work part time for the Air Force. They train one weekend a month and serve two full weeks each year. Nearly 250,000 people serve in the Air Force Reserves. These people can be called to active duty in emergencies.

The Air Force uses aircraft to protect the United States.

Air Force mechanics make sure equipment works properly.

Air Bases

Most U.S. Air Force members work at Air Force bases (AFBs). These bases may be in the United States or in another country.

Many Air Force members work overseas. More than 30,000 Air Force members work in

Europe. Some of them are stationed at bases in Germany and Great Britain. Nearly 25,000 Air Force members work in Asian countries. More than 8,000 Air Force members work in the Middle East and Africa.

Air Force Jobs

About 12,000 Air Force members are pilots. These officers fly airplanes and helicopters. Pilots use aircraft to attack enemy targets with bombs and missiles. Pilots also use aircraft to carry people and supplies where they are needed.

Air Force members perform other duties. Navigators use instruments to direct the flight of aircraft. Controllers use radar to guide pilots. Radar uses radio waves to locate distant objects. Air Force mechanics fix aircraft and equipment. Aerial gunners load weapons. Air Force doctors take care of wounded or sick Air Force members.

Some Air Force members train for special duties. Pararescue team members perform search-and-rescue missions. They find and help pilots whose planes have crashed. Combat controllers sneak into enemy territory. They set up landing areas for U.S. and allied aircraft.

CHAPTER 2

Learn about:

- **Early aircraft**

- **World wars**

- **The F-86 Sabre**

Hot-air balloons were the first aircraft used by the U.S. military.

Air Force History

Hot-air balloons were the first flying devices used by the U.S. military. Soldiers used these balloons to spy on enemy troops during the Civil War (1861–1865). Hot-air balloons lifted soldiers into the air. The soldiers then told their commanders what enemy troops were doing.

By 1907, the U.S. Army Signal Corps owned 10 hot-air balloons. This unit gathered information for the Army.

In 1909, the Army received its first airplane from Wilbur and Orville Wright. These brothers had invented the airplane six years earlier.

World War I

In World War I (1914–1918), the Allied forces fought against the Central Powers. Great Britain and France led the Allied forces. Germany and Austria-Hungary led the Central Powers.

In 1917, the United States joined the Allied forces. U.S. Army Air Service pilots fought in mid-air battles called dogfights. The Allied forces won the war in 1918.

World War II

In World War II (1939–1945), the Allied forces fought against the Axis powers. The Allied forces included the United States, the Soviet Union, France, and Great Britain. The Axis powers included Italy, Germany, and Japan.

Airplanes became more important during this war. U.S. pilots used fighter planes to attack enemy airplanes. They used bombers to drop bombs on enemy targets. Other planes carried paratroopers. These soldiers parachuted from airplanes into enemy areas.

In 1945, World War II ended. The Axis powers surrendered.

Pilots used aircraft to bomb enemy targets during World War II.

After the war, U.S. military leaders realized the importance of a strong Air Force. Military leaders felt that the Air Force should be a separate branch of the military. In 1947, Congress created the U.S. Air Force.

14 U.S. pilots used F-86 Sabres during the Korean War.

The Korean War

The Air Force first used jet fighters during the Korean War (1950–1953). This war began when North Korean troops invaded South Korea. The United States supported South Korea. China and the Soviet Union supported North Korea.

Chinese pilots flew Soviet-made MiG-15 fighter jets. These fighters were the best fighter jets at the time. The U.S. military developed F-86 Sabres to combat MiG-15s. Sabres were powerful jet fighters. Sabre pilots shot down nearly 800 enemy planes during the war. Only 58 Sabres were shot down.

The Vietnam War

Air Force pilots battled North Vietnamese MiG pilots during the Vietnam War (1954–1975). The United States helped South Vietnamese forces defend themselves against North Vietnamese forces during this war.

U.S. pilots used many types of aircraft during this war. F-4 Phantom pilots fired missiles at enemy targets. B-52 pilots dropped bombs on enemy targets.

CHAPTER 3

Learn about:

- **The Gulf War**

- **Aid to Somalia**

- **U.N. forces in Bosnia**

Air Force pilots played an important role in many recent conflicts.

Recent Conflicts

The role of the U.S. Air Force has changed since 1947. For more than 40 years, its main mission was to protect the United States from the Soviet Union. The Soviet Union opposed the United States in many conflicts. These conflicts included the Korean War and the Vietnam War.

In 1991, the Soviet Union broke apart into Russia and several smaller countries. U.S. military leaders believe that these countries are not as great of a threat to the United States. The Air Force now performs many smaller missions around the world.

The Gulf War

In 1991, more than 55,000 Air Force members took part in the Gulf War. This war was fought mainly through air attacks. U.S. pilots bombed enemy targets. They destroyed Iraqi missile launch sites, communication centers, and military buildings. They attacked ground troops. U.S pilots also destroyed 36 Iraqi aircraft during the war.

Air Force members performed many duties during the war. Some pilots flew supplies and troops where they were needed. Controllers kept track of the airplanes that were taking off and landing. Pararescue members rescued pilots whose planes crashed during the war.

The Gulf War ended after 43 days of fighting. Iraqi forces left Kuwait in early March.

Aid to Somalia

In 1992, U.S. leaders sent troops to Somalia. These troops were sent to help starving people in this African country. The U.S. military's actions were called Operation Restore Hope and Operation Continue Hope.

Air Force members performed many duties during these operations. Pilots flew troops and supplies to areas that were difficult to reach by truck. Air Force doctors cared for sick Somalians. The Air Force also helped fight Somalian warlords. These military leaders prevented food from getting to the people.

Air Force pilots helped bomb enemy targets during the Gulf War.

Peacekeeping in Bosnia

In 1991, fighting broke out in Yugoslavia. This European country had split into several smaller republics. These countries included Croatia, Bosnia-Herzegovina, and Slovenia. The United Nations (U.N.) sent peacekeeping troops to the area. The U.N. represents many of the world's governments. This group tries to keep peace in the world. Air Force members were part of the U.N. peacekeeping forces.

Air Force members helped protect a "no fly" zone over Bosnia. Air Force pilots patrolled the skies over Bosnia. They prevented pilots from other countries from flying over the area. This action helped keep U.N. forces safe. It also allowed U.N. forces to provide people in the area with food and shelter.

In November 1995, a peace agreement was reached among the republics. But some U.N. forces stayed in the area to keep the region safe. Air Force pilots continued to protect the "no fly" zone.

Important Dates

1907—U.S. Army Signal Corps forms an Aeronautical Division; this unit uses hot-air balloons to gather information.

1914—World War I begins; the first U.S. planes arrive in France in 1917.

1939—World War II begins; the United States enters the war in 1941.

1941—U.S. Congress forms the Army Air Forces.

1947—U.S. Congress makes the Air Force a separate branch of the military.

1950—Korean War begins; Air Force develops the F-86 Sabre.

1954—Vietnam War begins; the United States starts sending troops to Vietnam in the early 1960s.

1969—Air Force Colonel Edwin "Buzz" Aldrin becomes the second person to walk on the moon.

1981—The F-117A Nighthawk is flown for the first time.

1989—The B-2 Stealth bomber is flown for the first time.

1991—The Gulf War begins.

1992—Operation Restore Hope begins in Somalia.

B-2 Spirit

Function: Bomber

Manufacturer: Northrop Grumman Corporation

Date Deployed: 1993

Length: 69 feet (20.9 meters)

Wingspan: 171 feet (52.1 meters)

Speed: Classified

Range: 6,000 miles (9,655 kilometers)

The B-2 Spirit is a stealth bomber. This aircraft is designed to avoid radar. Radar sends out radio waves to locate distant objects. Radio waves bounce off objects and then return to the radar device. The B-2 Spirit's curved body is designed to scatter these waves. The B-2's body also is made from carbon fiber. This man-made material does not reflect radio waves as strongly as metals do.

The B-2's first test flight was in 1989. The Air Force received its first B-2 in 1993. This plane was called the *Spirit of Missouri*. The Air Force now has 21 B-2 Bombers.

B-2 Bombers were first used by the Air Force in 1999. Pilots flew B-2s over Serbia in eastern Europe. They bombed Serbian targets. These targets included bridges, railroads, power plants, and military buildings.

CHAPTER 4

Learn about:

- Space projects

- The F-22 Raptor

- The B-2 Spirit

The B-2 Spirit is a modern Air Force bomber.

Today's Air Force

The Air Force has served an important role in many recent conflicts. Air Force pilots have dropped bombs on enemy targets. They have delivered food and medicine to people. They also have protected people from attack by enemy forces. The Air Force develops new equipment to help its members continue performing these duties.

Air and Space

The Air Force helps develop space projects. Some Air Force officers train to become astronauts. They train at the National Aeronautics and Space Administration's (NASA) astronaut candidate training school.

Air Force pilots have flown to the moon. In 1969, Colonel Edwin "Buzz" Aldrin became the second person to walk on the moon. Air Force pilots also have flown in space shuttles.

Satellites

The Air Force uses satellites that circle Earth. Some satellites help people predict the weather. Information about the weather helps pilots plan missions. People also can send radio signals through satellites. These signals allow pilots to communicate with people at their headquarters or other locations.

Information gathered by satellites can tell Air Force members where enemy forces are located. During the Gulf War, pictures from the Navstar satellite system helped B-52 pilots locate enemy targets. Pilots dropped bombs on enemy targets from these airplanes.

Women in the Air Force

About 65,000 women serve in the Air Force. Women perform many of the same duties that men do. They may be officers or airmen.

Congressional law does not allow women to take part in ground combat specialties. These jobs may need to be performed while under direct fire from enemy forces.

In 1993, Congressional law first allowed women to fly combat aircraft. Since then, several women have trained to fly jet fighters.

Women also train to be astronauts. In 1999, Air Force Colonel Eileen Collins (left) became the first woman to command a space shuttle mission.

New Equipment

The Air Force is developing new airplanes to use in the future. The F-22 Raptor jet fighter is a stealth airplane.

Radar cannot easily locate stealth airplanes. Radar locates objects by sending out radio waves. These waves then bounce off objects and return to the radar device. The F-22's body is built at angles that scatter radio waves. The radio waves then do not return to the radar device. The Air Force plans to begin using this airplane in 2003.

The B-2 Spirit is a stealth bomber. The B-2 can carry nuclear weapons. These bombs use nuclear fission to create large explosions. Fission is the splitting of small particles called atoms.

The Air Force is designing defense systems for use in space. The Airborne Laser System will be able to shoot down missiles. This system uses high-energy beams of light to destroy enemy missiles.

The Air Force uses information gathered from satellites in space. Some satellites have cameras that can take pictures of enemy forces.

The F-22 Raptor is a new aircraft that the Air Force is testing.

This information helps military leaders plan missions. With new technology, the Air Force will continue to defend the United States.

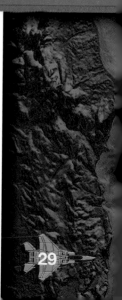

Words to Know

allies (AL-eyes)—people, groups, or countries that work together for a common cause

enlisted member (en-LIST-id MEM-bur)—a member of the Air Force who is not an officer; enlisted members also are called airmen.

fission (FISH-uhn)—the splitting of small particles called atoms; atoms are the tiniest part of a substance.

mission (MISH-uhn)—a military task

officer (OF-uh-sur)—an Air Force member who directs airmen in their duties

radar (RAY-dar)—equipment that uses radio waves to locate or guide objects

satellite (SAT-uh-lite)—a spacecraft that orbits the Earth

smart bomb (SMART BOM)—a bomb that can be aimed at enemy targets as it falls

stealth (STELTH)—built to avoid enemy radar; the F-22 Raptor is a stealth jet fighter; the B-2 Spirit is a stealth bomber.

To Learn More

Covert, Kim. *U.S. Air Force Special Forces: Pararescue.* Warfare and Weapons. Mankato, Minn.: Capstone High-Interest Books, 2000.

Green, Michael. *The United States Air Force.* Serving Your Country. Mankato, Minn.: Capstone High-Interest Books, 1998.

Holden, Henry M. *Air Force Aircraft.* Aircraft. Berkeley Heights, N.J.: Enslow, 2001.

Useful Addresses

Air Force Public Affairs Office
1690 Air Force Pentagon
Washington, DC 20330-1690

U.S. Air Force Museum
1100 Spaatz Street
Wright-Patterson AFB, OH 45433

Internet Sites

Air Force Link Jr.

http://www.af.mil/aflinkjr

U.S. Air Force

http://www.airforce.com

U.S. Air Force Museum

http://www.wpafb.af.mil/museum

Index

B-2 Spirit, 28
B-52, 15, 26

Civil War, 11

F-4 Phantom, 15
F-22 Raptor, 28
F-86 Sabre, 15
F-117A Nighthawk,
    5, 6

Gulf War, 5, 18, 26

Korean War, 15, 17

Operation Restore
    Hope, 18

satellites, 26, 28–29

U.S. Army Signal
    Corps, 11

Vietnam War, 15, 17

World War I, 12
World War II, 12